Anonymous

Fort-La-Fayette-Life

1863-64

Anonymous

Fort-La-Fayette-Life
1863-64

ISBN/EAN: 9783744754958

Printed in Europe, USA, Canada, Australia, Japan

Cover: Foto ©ninafisch / pixelio.de

More available books at **www.hansebooks.com**

1863–64

IN EXTRACTS FROM

THE "RIGHT FLANKER,"

\[MANU\]SCRIPT SHEET CIRCULATING AMONG THE SOUTHERN PRISONERS IN FORT-LA-FAYETTE, IN 1863–64.

•

Dedicated to them generally, and especially to the Confederate Officers whose autographs are here given, as among them were contributors to the "Right Flanker."

𝔏𝔬𝔫𝔡𝔬𝔫
SIMPKIN, MARSHALL & CO.
LIVERPOOL: EDWARD HOWELL.
1865.

CONTENTS.

PAGE

The Purpose in Starting the "Right Flanker"—The Antecedents of those with whom it originated ... 7

Arrival of Four Prisoners from New York—Their Antecedents—What they have really done, and what the Papers say they have done—What some of them think of our Cause in New York—Difference between a Confederate and a New York Peace Democrat: the latter believes in Governor Seymour; the former has no confidence in either him or Fernando Wood—Treatment of Prisoners, October 1863 15

The effect which sending down four at a time had among the Free Whites of New York—Dangerous to have a Life of Stonewall Jackson in the House, or to have a Package directed to Fort-la-Fayette.. 23

Close Confinement, for an Attempt to Escape—Additional Restrictions on account of an Old Knife—Lady Friend Visitors—Recollections of Baltimoreans 27

Contents.

	PAGE
Arrival of a distinguished Confederate Officer—Bouquets to Prisoners—Colonel Burke and a Prisoner on the War—The strict Lieutenant	29
Paroles withdrawn—More Restrictions on Prisoners—New York Illustrated Papers—Fighting among the Clouds—The Herald—Reliable Sheet—Bennett, Barnum, and Lincoln	33
Orders for Retaliation—Prisoners restricted to Garrison Fare—Rebels won't complain if it will serve to show the extremes to which a coercive Union Government is reduced—An addition to the Prisoners by an Officer in the British Army, for having Letters from Rebel Ladies—Visit to a Prisoner by a Union Friend: they had been betting on the Capture of Richmond by M'Clellan, and the Recognition of the Confederacy by England and France	37
Winter Weather—Gloomy Feelings brightened by the Cheseapeake affair, and News from the Alabama—A Rebel, an English Officer, and Colonel Burke as to Special Privileges—A Chair allowed the English Officer	43
Quite a Number of Additional Prisoners—Rules more Strict—A British Shipmaster confined with Negroes	45
New Year—More Prisoners—Another British Officer, an Envoy Extraordinary to Washington,	

Contents.   iii.
PAGE

and Secretary, captured by order of Mr. Seward—The Wife and Daughter of the Minister in the Station House—Several New York Merchants brought down; they have plenty of money, and expect to be out soon—Old Prisoners don't think they will 49

The Arrival of a former New York Hotel Keeper, lately engaged in raising a Regiment of Soldiers—An Admirer of Ladies presenting Flags to Negroes instead of White Men—Prevalence of Neuralgia and Toothache: services of a Dentist denied—Running the Blockade—Butter in Cell No. 3 51

Interesting Reading—Contents of a Rebel Mail, which affords the first idea to some of the Prisoners as to the Cause of their Arrest—One of Mr. Seward's Despatches among Rebel Prisoners in Fort-la-Fayette and Baltimore Rebel Ladies—More Lady Visitors to the Fort—"The Bonnie Blue Flag," and "I love Old Dixie, right or wrong," by Prisoners 55

Excitement in consequence of a Vessel attempting to Pass before being Examined—More Loyal Citizens brought down as Prisoners—Additional Restrictions as to Visitors—The Blockade Run with Greenbacks for Prisoners—Trading them with Yankee Soldiers—Successful Strategy in getting New Clothes 59

Contents.

More Prisoners—Financial Operation between a Prisoner and the United States Authorities—The (supposed) Head of the Soldier-defrauding Fraternity brought down—He is thoroughly Union, and Elected a Member of Congress, who is to get him out—Invitation to Yankees found in the South when the War is over............................ 65

Arrival of a Military Commission for Trial of Prisoners — Additional Restrictions — Orders for Visitors to be Searched—Officer's Object, Order Withdrawn—Excitement in the Fort—Anticipated Attempt to Release Prisoners—Neither Catholic Newspapers nor Episcopal Prayer Books allowed—Proceedings of the Military Commission—How a New York Silver-grey Democrat wanted to Bet—What a Jersey Democrat would be glad to hear—Discharge of British Subjects—The Yankee Policy as to British Blockade Runners. 69

Removal of Confederate Officers to another Fort—Two escape on the way—Anticipated Departure of Two others for their Homes: Entertainment in their Honour—Editorial Banquet of the "Right Flanker"—The Sensation of the Day: "Braves, who have with Stonewall Bled!" for the First Time... 77

A trifling article denied a Prisoner—News from the Escaped Prisoners—One has a pleasant time in

Contents. v.

PAGE

Western Virginia, Baltimore, New York, and Boston, before leaving for Bermuda—Leaving of Two Prisoners for Fortress Monroe, to be Exchanged—The proceedings of the Military Commission concluded—The only result the Transfer of a rich Union Citizen to a New York Jail 87

The Military Commissioners and a Confederate Engineer; the latter contends that there is a Confederate Government, for which he is more closely Locked up—A Jar of Oysters denied a Prisoner. 91

A Union Prisoner's Appeal for Vegetables—His Relatives fear that his Mind is Affected—His hope on account of Rothschilds' Agent hanging out the Old Flag, and helping to Crush the Rebellion—Controversies between Northern Citizens as to the Standard for Society—Difference of Treatment to Union and Rebel Prisoners. ... 93

The Strong Arms and Brave Hearts of their Countrymen the only Dependence of Rebel Prisoners—Anticipated necessity for Discontinuance of the "Right Flanker"—Removal of several Prisoners from the Fort, and the existing Copies of it entrusted to them—Final Discontinuance of it—Publication of Fort-la-Fayette Life. 97

FORT-LA-FAYETTE LIFE.

THE PURPOSE IN STARTING THE "RIGHT FLANKER"
—THE ANTECEDENTS OF THOSE WITH WHOM
IT ORIGINATED.

IN starting such a sheet as the "Right Flanker," the purpose is to relieve the monotony of prison life, by calling into action the taste and faculties of those who are capable of contributing to its columns; instructing and amusing those who cannot, and to furnish to all who are to share the spice of excitement, which the risk of such a contraband undertaking affords, something of which, it is hoped, reference can be pleasantly made by them in after years.

It being concluded that all interested should be properly introduced to each other, it is mutually understood that the parties having the duties of the editorial staff to assume, have authority to do it as they think proper; and it occurs to them, that no plan will be more interesting than that of making each other correctly aware of their respective antecedents.

The commencement is with the oldest prisoner in the fort, the party who is to attend to the agricultural department of the "Right Flanker."

A young Virginia farmer volunteered his services among the earliest, in the defence of his native soil, served his time out, and returned home, to find the old homestead destroyed by the invaders; was denounced as a guerilla for endeavouring to save a family relic; hunted by a detachment of some sixty Yankee soldiers, who surrounded the house in which he took refuge; with the assistance of the ladies, kept the enemy at bay for some time, but was finally captured, confined in the lower hold of a three-decked iron-clad for two months, in midsummer, heavily ironed both hand and foot; his arrival in New York chronicled as that of the most notorious character; and delivered in Fort-la-Fayette as the most savage rebel as yet inside its walls.

Next in order is an adventurer from his native place, Nova Scotia, to North Carolina; piloted on that coast as long as there was anything to do in that line; since then he may have tried the sailing qualities of a Baltimore-built pilot boat, in coming up with a Yankee craft, in a way disagreeable to her skipper; still he was quietly located at a New York hotel, when he was ordered to care of Colonel Burke, until efforts could be made to find something against him. As he writes a good letter to Lord Lyons occasionally, in consequence of his not having been naturalized, he is to be known as the diplomatic head of the "Right Flanker."

Then follows the party who is to be looked to as the nautical reporter—a young Confederate officer. He is, as all agree he should be, estimated as one, if not the most brave in our gallant little navy. Eight months in Fort Warren, for being proof against the temptation of money and place to forswear his allegiance to his native South, did not prevent him from taking, as it were, his life in his hand; and the indignities and suffering which he has had to bear from his captors since *he was found under the bottom of the Ironside,* would be considered as nothing, if he could look back to the result, had he got just eighteen inches further down under that celebrated vessel.

Then we have a true representative of the jolly boatmen of the Alabama; he does not despair of again giving the familiar notice of his approach (the shrill note of the steam whistle) to the little family on its banks; he is here the victim of a Pensylvanian, who was navigator of a blockade runner, but who got off by paying the captors of her to substitute for him a person who had never been on the water, except as a pilot on the Alabama river. He is evidently thinking of his man when he comes to that part of his favourite song which says,—

"The Sixteenth Lousiana charged them with a yell,"
"Bagged the Bucktail Rangers, and sent them all to ——."

Another case of Yankee victimising is in a Georgian, to whom a New Yorker by adoption, but Yankee by birth, having held the position of a confidential friend in the South, and came from there with him, was intrusted with the care of a considerable amount of money. After reaching New York, the result was, that not only did the Yankee practice the 'cute trick (it is not usual to use a harsher term in Yankeedom in respect of operations of the kind) of holding on to all the money, but reporting that it was intended for purchasing contraband of war, had him, who had often befriended him in Georgia, locked up here.

The appointed local item reporter with a blockade runner, in which he had considerable property, fell into the clutches of a Federal cruiser when homeward bound to the place which, according to the New York papers, has been, since the war commenced, totally destroyed at least three times, but still a pile of bricks reminds the Yankees so much of *Sumter* that, as yet, they cannot witness the ruins of the hated city. He hears that the invaders have left him without a home, but he has the satisfaction of remembering that he had his share of the glory of being one of the few who lessened their numbers so rapidly at Secessionville.

The Chess reporting is confided to the most

quiet of the inmates of cell No. 3, who, if he had not conceived the idea of putting the machinery of a lumber-mill (which was of no use in consequence of the blockade) near Mobile into a schooner of his, would not be among us.

The land-o'-cakes is represented amongst us by a person who assumes the place of musical contributor. It is to be hoped that he will do justice to the romance which he attaches to his own case—from the numerous escapes he made while fighting among the rebels, to fall into the Yankee trap while in the enjoyment of ladies' society, when on his way home from Dixie. In vain he tells Lord Lyons that he was passing through the Federal territory in no other than the character of an honourably discharged Confederate officer, but to no purpose: Mr. Seward has to be believed first, and it suits him to have him held as a spy.

The idea of a person who, until the breaking out of hostilities—whose whole interest lay in fast boats and large loads of cotton on the Mississippi and the Alabama—represents some half-a-dozen among the readers of the " Right Flanker;" the remainder of the number who are present is made up by a person who, on account of his father having fought under the old Napoleon, has faith that, as soon as his case is plainly represented, the younger one will take it up, the result of which will be not only his immediate release, but the winning of a bet from his English-born shipmate, who, at the time of the capture of the blockade runner in which they were together, backed his opinion that the British Lion was no more afaid than the French Eagle of the Yankee scare-crow.

A silver-haired person, whose offence was the feeding of the furnaces of a blockade runner, but who rejoices in not having been guilty of doing more than declaring his intention to formally renounce his allegiance to the country which gave him birth. A Yankee who had been acting as an officer of a British steamer, seized when on the point of leaving New York on suspicion of being intended for the blockade business, and another under miliary arrest, for complicity, as sergeant of a quarter-master, in defrauding the United States, completes the present party in Fort-la-Fayette, with the exception of one who is in close confinement on the charge of having been at the head of the rioters in New York a short time since; what is to be known of him is, that his case is the result of the taste which has too often induced young men to prefer the imaginary pleasure of life in the commercial metropolis, to the real ones of Southern hospitality. He is a Virginian.

The fine October weather continues; still, on account of the quarters allotted us having become too crowded, the heat at night is very trying in a close cell. In the eating line we get along pretty well—more than half of us rebels having means enough in the hands of the adjutant of the fort to procure something additional to soldiers' fare for ourselves and the others; and the friends of the loyal citizens—which term covers all brought here (no matter for what) who do not strictly come under the head of actual rebels or their sympathisers—are at liberty to supply them.

ARRIVAL OF FOUR PRISONERS FROM NEW YORK—
THEIR ANTECEDENTS — WHAT THEY HAVE
REALLY DONE, AND WHAT THE PAPERS SAY
THEY HAVE DONE — WHAT SOME OF THEM
THINK OF OUR CAUSE IN NEW YORK — DIF-
FERENCE BETWEEN A CONFEDERATE AND A
NEW YORK PEACE DEMOCRAT: THE LATTER
BELIEVES IN GOVERNOR SEYMOUR; THE FOR-
MER HAS NO CONFIDENCE IN EITHER HIM OR
FERNANDO WOOD—TREATMENT OF PRISONERS,
OCTOBER 1863.

THIS week has brought quite an addition, and, according to appearance, an important one, to our number, as much on account of the evidence afforded of the probable course of things at the North, as on account of one of the parties having had, as a friend of the Southern cause, continual experience in New York since the breaking out of hostilities. He is accompanied by another Marylander, of his own feelings, a New Jersey and a New York citizen, both of whom intimate that they prefer being looked upon as Peace Democrats. They shall be estimated as such; at the same time, as the idea current among us is that all who are not for us are against us, they cannot expect to be considered as having taken the higher order.

The newspapers which we are allowed to purchase (any but those advocating the war or Administration are prohibited) give all kinds of versions to their cases, more particularly as to the principal one of our Maryland friends; one of them (the papers) having it that he was in the habit of making Republican speeches while acting the part of a rebel emissary; another has him a dealer in torpedoes; a third a confidential travelling agent for Mr. Vallandigham while in Dixie; while a fourth would have him held to a strict account for having had in his office some boxes which, from their weight, must have contained something contraband. All agree as to the importance of his captured corespondence, and promise their readers rich developments. One editor, no doubt wishing to be ahead of all competitors, tells his patrons that the arrest proved to be of much greater importance than at first supposed, although, after having made enquiries at the Marshal's office, he failed to elicit anything new in regard to them.

The true particulars are noted as follows: A Yankee, who had been in the confidence of parties in Baltimore as a Virginian in the Potomac blockade business, became a Washington War Department Detective Officer, from which department he was supplied with funds for the purpose of making purchases of articles, contraband of war, from his former friends in Baltimore, and then got an introduction through them to their New York confidants, with the avowed purpose of getting assistance in procuring passage from thence to Richmond with articles much needed by the authorities there.

The plan, unfortunately for our Maryland friend, worked but too well. As soon as he had sufficiently committed himself, and the contraband articles were in his charge, the United States Secretary of War issued an order for his arrest, and instructed the officer making the arrest to deliberately deceive his prisoner by an assurance that he was merely required for an hour at a Provost Marshal's office ; and he did not undeceive him until he had got him outside the limits of the City of New York.

The other Marylander comes compromised as master of the vessel, which it is charged was to have taken the supposed Confederate to Virginia.

Our greyheaded room-mate was engaged by the detective to negotiate the purchase, from his New Jersey friend, of some patent fusé, also for the use of the Confederate Government. As the ideas of these gentlemen are of interest, as evidence of what is going on in this part of the Lincoln dominion, they are noted. The principal of our Maryland friends, from having held the position of a confidential Southern sympathiser from the first, and from the fact that it has been but a few weeks since he was last threatened, has more to complain of, from the means resorted to in making the arrest, than from the arrest itself. He has been, as it might be said, inside the scenes ever since the exposing of a name on the face of a card, instead of the one upon its back, in all probability decided the fate of Fortress Monroe at the commencement of the war. It is his belief that, outside of the few in New York who contend that *Southern Independence should be a right, not a concession*, we have not any friends, unless they are to be considered as such, who are in opposition to the present war-making power, merely for the purpose of trying to secure the advantage of place and power to carry it on themselves. The cases of two leading New York lawyers, who but a short time since would let the "wayward sisters" go in peace, is pretty strong proof that he is right. Our greyheaded room-mate dissents from that view, and estimates that there are many thousands prepared unhesitatingly to make peace on the basis of Southern Independence; but he believes in Governor Seymour. Our Maryland friend has no confidence in either Seymour or Fernando Wood. Our New Jersey room-mate is, like most inventors, so completely absorbed in the idea of astonishing the rest of mankind, that with the exception of claiming to be considered as an old time Democrat, he allows little to trouble him, but the possible result of his arrest on the fate of the "endless chain of Fire," as he calls his patent fusé. He was on the point of arranging to let the Government at Washington have its advantages, for the destruction of whole rebel armies at one time; but as he and the Federal General, who was to have had a share of the profit, disagreed as to the amount he was to have, he became willing to dispose of the invention to any other party; and as it turned up, a War Department Detective came along as another party. The chances are very unfavourable to his realizing anything from the project, which has been his study for several years. The Detective was to have secured him in a quarter of a million dollars, if his (the Detective's) plan for introducing the invention into the Southern Confederacy had succeeded. Our Jersey acquaintance considers that it was not his place to require an explanation from a purchaser of his fusé as to what was to be done with it, which was quite reasonable in our opinion, as we see that his State is perfectly careless as to the use to which her soldiers are put in the prosecution of the war. They don't object to be ordered to burn a house, or take a piano belonging to their former friends, in the South.

On account of our Maryland friend having become acquainted with Colonel Burke some time since, while a visitor to a Baltimore friend of his, then in charge of the Colonel for giving currency to the report that General M'Clellan had retreated to Harrison Landing, or from the fact that the daughters of both had been school-mates in Maryland, or perhaps from the Colonel and himself being of the same religious persuasion, the Colonel appears inclined to prefer that our Maryland friend should be the person to treat with him on the part of the prisoners in general, to which we unanimously agree. Already, from representation by him, the Colonel has been induced to give orders for the fitting up of new quarters, to which it is intended to remove some of the prisoners from each cell, thereby adding to the general comfort; and Southern friends of his in New York have been written to by him in respect to the wants of several in the way of clothing.

THE EFFECT WHICH SENDING DOWN FOUR AT A TIME HAD AMONG THE FREE WHITES OF NEW YORK—DANGEROUS TO HAVE A LIFE OF STONEWALL JACKSON IN THE HOUSE, OR TO HAVE A PACKAGE DIRECTED TO FORT-LA-FAYETTE.

NOTHING of special interest to us occurred this week, except as regards the case of our Maryland friend. His friends in New York have given proof that they not only desire that he should want for nothing in their power to afford, under existing circumstances, but also of their readiness to meet the suggestions made by him as to the necessities of some of his fellow prisoners. His daughter was permitted by Col. Day, in command of Fort Hamilton, to come over to this Fort; but Col. Burke would not allow her an interview with him, in the absence of a permit from higher authority. He, however, has learned something of the effect caused by his arrest. It appears to have extended from the case of those who have been in the habit of visiting his office, to the domestics in the family with whom he resided—the former having become afraid to enter the office; and the latter, in the absence of the family, would not rest easy whilst the least evidence of his sympathies remained in the house. A life of Stonewall Jackson was carried to the hayloft; all the letters and papers found in his office have been sent to the War Department. There is an extensive field for speculation as to the effect of examination of the contents of the former, as they include correspondence from a variety of persons, extending to even letters from schoolgirls; but fortunately, nothing has been found as proof of his connection with any one in the Rebel States, or of his having sent goods there. He has surprised the adjutant by taking advantage of the privilege to order such of the administration papers as he prefers, in selecting an extreme abolition Sheet, the *Tribune*, for the reason as he gives, that the Editor is an open and consistent enemy, as such, and as a fanatic, an advocate of the war; while his War Democratic contemporaries are quite as much for Southern subjugation, but, from being less independent and consistent, are less honourable.

While on the subject of independence in New York, it is to be noted that the proprietor of three of the principal restaurants there, objected to a package containing some game, being directed in his premises to a prisoner here.

CLOSE CONFINEMENT, FOR AN ATTEMPT TO ESCAPE—
ADDITIONAL RESTRICTIONS ON ACCOUNT OF AN
OLD KNIFE—LADY FRIEND VISITORS—RECOL-
LECTIONS OF BALTIMOREANS.

THE most interesting events of the week have been the removal from Cell No. 3 to close confinement, of our friend from Georgia, and the withdrawal from the prisoners who have been removed to new quarters, of the privilege of eating their rations in their cells. The first in consequence of a charge that he had attempted to procure a life-preserving suit in order to escape, and the latter in consequence of the Colonel, while excited about this finding a knife which he suspected had been purposely gapped to be used as a saw, to cut the bars of one of the cell windows. They now have to eat where, when and as fast as the soldiers do, or get no garrison fare.

As any of us who are fortunate enough to hear at all from our home ties, only get what can be communicated by the half-letter sheet, per flag of truce, we congratulate our Maryland friend on the success of his daughter in procuring a pass to visit him twice a-week. Her appearance is appreciated not only on account of its serving to freshen the recollection of many of us of the time we were made to feel so much at home in the Monumental city, but also on account of her frequent visits to the Fort, pleasantly reminding us, that we are not forgotten by the fair sex. While upon the subject of Baltimore and its ladies, it is to be noted that a friend there has contributed to our comfort already, and our young lady friend and her companion invariably think of *us all*, when bringing delicacies with them. "God bless old Maryland."

Arrival of a distinguished Confederate Officer — Bouquets to Prisoners — Colonel Burke and a Prisoner on the war—The strict Lieutenant.

THE events which come under our heading of historic for this week are the addition to the inmates of Cell No. 3, of a gentleman, in regard to whom we all most feelingly adopt the expression (of no doubt an honest Hibernian, and who may have been a rebel) that we are "most sorry and glad" to meet, a worthy representative of him whose name alone attracts the attention of those who can appreciate true patriotism and chivalry, wherever the cause of the South is known. Our Baltimore lady friends made their appearance as usual, and we are glad to find them report favourably as to the care of them by the boatmen, and the considerate attention on the part of the officers, whose place it has been to be present at their interviews with the object of their visits. We are not indebted to them only this week, as in the windows of both Cells 2 and 3, are displayed bouquets, marks of appreciation on the part of a lady residing in sight of the Fort, of the newly-arrived rebel general and the rebel naval officer within its walls. Since our Georgian friend's removal to close confinement, our Maryland friend has been in his place as caterer for No. 3 Mess, the consequence is, that between the occasions, he has to make on that account, to meet the officers at their quarters, and those he makes on account of his lady visitors, he has frequent opportunities of a friendly exchange of opinion with them (the officers). In the last, the Colonel thought Mr. Davis a very able and ambitious man, but he had now attempted to do too much. Our Maryland friend remarking that, *as yet, there were no signs of the rebellion being crushed.* As a matter of course, they (the officers) are of but one opinion as to the result of the struggle, doubtless if that was other than that numbers and money are bound to succeed, some of them would not have concluded to risk their lives in soldiering. So far, with the exception of one, the junior officers appear to correctly appreciate their duty in regard to prisoners. The Colonel, on account of age, is entitled to some allowance; but we have none for the young man, who takes pleasure in making it evident that he is expert in the duties of a jailer, more especially, as we have reason to believe, that he cannot have been long away from his native country, where jails and jailers are so dreaded. The idea of bouquets to rebels is mortifying to his feelings, and already he complains of the extra trouble from an examination of the contents of an increased number of packages for the prisoners, even though it is caused by the approach of the general feasting time—Thanksgiving.

Paroles withdrawn — More Restrictions on Prisoners—New York Illustrated. Papers —Fighting among the Clouds—The Herald —Reliable Sheet—Bennett, Barnum, and Lincoln.

THE fine weather, and the extra enjoyment of the good things of life, which thanksgiving day brought, made the week pass comparatively more pleasant. We have had an addition to the inmates of No. 3, in the person of a Confederate officer, captured in hospital at the surrender of Vicksburg, paroled there, and brought to New York. The newspapers clamouring for retaliation on rebel prisoners in the North, for the supposed bad treatment of Union captives in the South, the commanding General ignored his parole, and sent him down here. In more than this it is evident that there is going to be a tightening of the screws, as a sentinel has been posted between us and the former inmates of No. 2 and 3, who have been removed to the other side of the Fort, having come under the ban of the Colonel on account of the old knife with the gapped edge. Our Maryland friend can't persuade the Colonel that the position in which his (the Colonel's) cook found it, was not the consequence of an effort on the part of the prisoners to make it answer the purpose of a refined steel saw, although it would not require the judgment of a person more experienced in the use of steel than from all accounts he (the Colonel) is, to ascertain that the article which has so troubled him could not be successfully used in cutting a harder substance than the beef in Fort-la-Fayette.

Our Maryland lady friends made their accustomed visits. In addition to how much we read in the newspapers about Grant in the neighbourhood of Lookout Mountain, we are allowed to see efforts in illustrated prints to impress us with the idea of how General Hooker had been fighting among the clouds. Of course the rebels are represented as in the dissolving views, and as a coincidence, we presume, Bennett of the *Herald* feels warranted in departing from his policy of not attempting to prematurely offer an opinion as to events in the future, by coming squarely out in assuring his readers that the crushing of the rebellion by New Year is a settled thing. The readers no doubt imagine that it is the next New Year that he means. Nothing of the kind, for, should it be ten years until the war ceases, and Bennett lives so long, we are willing to wager that following that event, an article will be noticed in the *New York Herald* taking credit for its foresight in predicting the close of hostilities at just that time. If we were New Yorkers we would of course say, "Give us Humbug," and of course that could not be done without Bennett and Barnum were included. As rebels, we prefer Bennett and Lincoln being together.

ORDERS FOR RETALIATION—PRISONERS RESTRICTED TO GARRISON FARE—REBELS WON'T COMPLAIN IF IT WILL SERVE TO SHOW THE EXTREMES TO WHICH A COERCIVE UNION GOVERNMENT IS REDUCED—AN ADDITION TO THE PRISONERS BY AN OFFICER IN THE BRITISH ARMY, FOR HAVING LETTERS FROM REBEL LADIES—VISIT TO A PRISONER BY A UNION FRIEND: THEY HAD BEEN BETTING ON THE CAPTURE OF RICHMOND BY M'CLELLAN, AND THE RECOGNITION OF THE CONFEDERACY BY ENGLAND AND FRANCE.

THE gloomy weather of the week has accorded with our feelings, in consequence of (we presume) the clamouring by the New York editors for retaliation on rebel prisoners having had the effect of inducing the Washington authorities to order that we be deprived of the privilege to either purchase or receive any articles whatever from outside the Fort, with the exception of writing materials, pipes, tobacco, and cigars, which are allowed to be purchased on our account. Our Maryland friend, and caterer for Mess No. 3, has had several interviews with the officers in regard to so unexpected a restriction, without being enabled to come to a conclusion other than that the influence of his Irish lieutenant, who has been so pointedly unfavourable to the prisoners in general, has induced Colonel Burke to make suggestions to the War Department, which on account of the existing state of public feeling the Secretary of War was prompt to avail of.

The officers directly in charge of us have been good enough to induce their Colonel to ask additional instructions with regard to his orders, the only favourable result of which is, that prisoners who have relatives (friends won't do) in New York, are at liberty to have them, furnish them with one change of under and over-clothes, and a pair of laced (not long-legs) boots. All other prisoners, whether with or without means to purchase, are obliged to accept the gratuity of the United States Government in furnishing them, the same as its own common soldiers. As soon as what remains of the abundance in the eating line from purchases on our own account at the village of Fort Hamilton, and donations by New York sympathisers, is consumed, our recourse will have to be solely to tough beef, dry bread, beans, and bad coffee. But let it come, many of us have done marching, and successful fighting, on still shorter rations; and if the 50,000 friends, which our greyheaded room-mate says are in New York ready to avenge any special indignity towards him, are merely gently admonished of the excesses to which their most benign Government is compelled to have recourse we rebels shall be particular not to complain, although we know that Federal prisoners were never denied the use of their own funds in the South, or to receive whatever was sent them by friends.

Our Maryland lady friends have been down as usual, and were much disgusted to find us under the new restriction, but from having found an old United States Officer to receive them, and explain matters, they went home in hopes of its being soon removed. We are of the opinion, that except the Colonel and his Irish Lieutenant, the officers on duty would prefer that matters should go on as heretofore.

The week has brought no change in favour of our comfort; the old campaigners among us have been exercising their ingenuity in making garrison fare more palatable to those unaccustomed to roughing it. Result favourable to the Rebel cause, as there is more emphatic language to be heard against their Government by those who heretofore would occasionally suggest the possibility of a restoration of the Union.

Cell No. 2 has had an addition to the number of its inmates in the person of a Lieutenant in H.M. service, and a Confederate Captain; the former captured under orders from Secretary Seward, on board of a British vessel when on the point of leaving New York for Bermuda. Charge: associating with disloyal ladies in Baltimore, and having on his person letters from them to parties in Bermuda, to be forwarded to Richmond. The latter, one of a number of the citizens of the Confederacy who were on board of a lately captured Blockade Runner. Some half-a-dozen others taken in company with him have arrived in the portion of the Fort to which we are now denied access, consequently we can merely ascertain that the most of them are gentlemen from South Carolina and Virginia.

Our Maryland friend has had a Union friend, with whom he has been domiciled ever since the War commenced, to visit him. It is presumed that the fact of this gentleman being a member of one of the New York Militia regiments accounts for the protracted interview he was allowed to have with a prisoner here. Our room-mate came back to his cell quite pleased, as the reference was principally to amusing occurrences, such as the betting between him and his Union friend on the capture of Richmond by McClellan, the recognition of the Confederacy by England and France, and the time when he was threatened with Fort-la-Fayette for expressing the opinion that Mason and Slidell should not have been arrested, by a person who afterwards made a similar threat when he expressed the opinion that they should not have been given up without a fight. His Union friend brings him also an idea as to the reason for the absence of such replies as he had been expecting to the communications sent to his friends in New York in regard to his case. It appears that they are alarmed at receiving so explanatory letters from a Fort-la-Fayette prisoner, fearing that the officer of the post, whose place it is to read them, is interested in getting as many persons as possible implicated. It is not so. The officers here would prefer that they should not be required to have charge of any prisoners.

Our Maryland lady friends have been down as usual, and from finding that there was no relaxation in the rules as to our treatment, have changed their views, so as to relieve the conscience of one of them (the younger) in regard to being the means of putting a letter from a husband in the Fort into the hands of a Southern wife without the examination of a Federal officer.

Winter Weather—Gloomy Feelings brightened by the Cheseapeake affair, and News from the Alabama — A Rebel, an English Officer, and Colonel Burke as to Special Privileges—A Chair allowed the English Officer.

Winter weather has been fairly initiated this week; the night to us now is nearly fifteen hours, counting from lock-up time to the opening of the cell in the morning. During it we lose patience with every kind of games which it is in our power to engage in, and we cannot raise a laugh at even the expatiation of the New York papers on the subject of whole brigades of rebels asking to be received within the Union lines on the Rapidan.

The capture of the Cheseapeake, and the late news of the doings of the Alabama, interest us; so does the speech of Fernando Wood in New Jersey. We wonder what his meaning was when he said: "Not another man or dollar for the prosecution of the war." Ben Wood of New York, Bayard of Delaware, and Harris of Maryland, are those *whom we estimate* as pointing to the Star of Peace.

The Confederate Captain brought here last week, having been reported by the New York papers as deserving of consideration on account of special kindness to Federal prisoners in Richmond, thought that he had better ascertain what effect such a character would have with Colonel Burke, by soliciting the privilege of procuring something in addition to the garrison fare. He failed in his purpose, as did the British officer in an effort on his part to impress the Colonel with an idea that he should not be treated as a common rebel. He has had H.M. Vice-Consul down from New York to intercede in his behalf, but without success, except as to allowing him a camp chair in his cell.

Our Maryland lady friends have not been deterred from their accustomed visits by the cold and stormy weather, and have succeeded in getting the privilege from some of the officers who are in the habit of being present at their interviews with our room-mate, to bring him sufficient to constitute an ordinary lunch, to be taken during the interview.

QUITE A NUMBER OF ADDITIONAL PRISONERS—RULES MORE STRICT—A BRITISH SHIPMASTER CONFINED WITH NEGROES.

THIS week has brought quite an addition to the prisoners of the Fort. On our side we have a Virginia Confederate Captain from the old Capitol, where he has been in solitary confinement for several months as a hostage for a Federal soldier reported to have been held as a hostage in Richmond. It now appears that it was all a mistake as to any Union soldier being ordered to be hung. (Had it been so ordered, it would have been done with despatch by the Confederate Government.) The addition to our neighbours in No. 2 is a young Georgia gentleman, who was paroled from here some months since, and brought back under the late retaliatory orders from Washington. To the numbers in the other part of the Fort have been added a General and Staff of the Confederate Army just from New Orleans. The Commander and Officers of a Confederate Blockade Runner. The Commander and Officers of a British Blockade Runner, and an

Irish merchant captured while passing through New York from Canada.

The rules are so strictly enforced as to keeping us in No. 2 and 3 separate from those in other quarters of the Fort, that we can only ascertain who they are by the knowledge our room-mates have of some of them personally, and the public reputation of those belonging to the Confederate Service. The latter, from having been some time under Federal control in New Orleans, make less complaint of unexpected restrictions to which they have become subject, but the Englishmen take it quite hard, especially the Captain, on account of being denied the consideration due his station, to assign him quarters separate from a crew made up of (not the most select) different nations, among whom are negroes.

Our lady friends down as usual, and succeeded, by permission of the officer of the day, in supplying the inmates of No. 3 with sufficient fresh meat to enable them to say that Christmas brought them a variety in the eating line. The mutton chops were much appreciated on account alone of the labour and exposure occasioned the ladies in getting over the ice to the boat. We hope that Lieutenant S—n may never be so situated as to enjoy, as some of us did, a small share of the contents of that little basket. The appearance of several one-limbed Confederate officers, endeavouring to get about over the ice covered space allotted them for exercise, makes our feelings at the setting in of cold weather additionally disagreeable.

New Year—More Prisoners—Another British Officer, an Envoy Extraordinary to Washington, and Secretary, captured by order of Mr. Seward — The Wife and Daughter of the Minister in the Station House — Several New York Merchants brought down; 'they have plenty of money and expect to be out soon—Old Prisoners don't think they will.

The commencement of 1864 has so added to the number of prisoners, that instead of about 20 two months ago, there must now be 100 more. The latest editions have been another British officer, An envoy extraordinary from a Central American Republic to Washington, and his secretary, a Spanish gentleman. They are not on our side of the Fort, but we are authorised to note their cases as follows:—The Envoy came to New York to purchase arms for the use of his Government, contracted with a manufacturer, who was to ship them in packages of lard to Cuba, (the exportation of them being prohibited.) As soon as on board ship, the detective comes along, seizes the property, sends the owner, secretary, and friend (the British officer) to care of Colonel Burke, and the wife and daughter of the Foreign Minister to a police station-house, where they were kept some time.

In addition to the foregoing, we have the cases of two British subjects and one English naturalized New York merchant: charges—shipping goods to a British port under fraudulent bonds, that they should not be sent to the Confederacy; collusion with an officer of the Custom House in passing the bonds; clearance of coal for Sicily, and having it landed at Nassau; and other contraband operations. They have means, and expect to get out at once. Old prisoners don't believe they can do it so easily. One of them (the old prisoners) wagers with a new comer that he won't be out in a week even if he has a couple of hundred thousand dollars at his back; it will take longer than that to ascertain how to work the wires.

THE ARRIVAL OF A FORMER NEW YORK HOTEL KEEPER, LATELY ENGAGED IN RAISING A REGIMENT OF SOLDIERS—AN ADMIRER OF LADIES PRESENTING FLAGS TO NEGROES INSTEAD OF WHITE MEN — PREVALENCE OF NEURALGIA AND TOOTHACHE: SERVICES OF A DENTIST DENIED — RUNNING THE BLOCKADE — BUTTER IN CELL NO. 3.

WE have a former New York hotel keeper, lately connected with a Federal Colonel in raising a regiment: charge—defrauding recruits of their bounty. None of the last three Englishmen come under the head of rebel sympathisers: they are favourable to the rebellion merely on account of the money they make out of it

The late hotel keeper acknowledges to be an admirer of the taste displayed within a few days by the leading wives and daughters of New York, in presenting a Negro Regiment with colours, and otherwise paying them more marked attention than any white Regiment that has gone to the war; and one of the British subjects does not hesitate to say that he is an Abolitionist.

Weather very cold. Toothaches and neuralgia prevalent in Cell No. 3. Our Maryland friend and the ladies have done all in their power towards getting permission for them to send down a dentist to operate in the presence of an officer : which privilege was denied.

Since restriction as to food, our young lady friend evinces a taste for the contraband by having butter in small pieces for placing in her father's pockets, whenever the officer of the day is not watching, and her father is eating his share of the contents of her little basket. Occasionally we get other palatable morsels in the same way. Lady friends of some of the prisoners, not knowing that doing so was forbidden, sent fowls and other eatables down for the New Year dinner. It was ordered that they be added to what was specially furnished on account of the Yankee Anniversary for that meal, which was required to be partaken of at a general table with the soldiers. Most of us in

Cells 2 and 3, as well as others, preferred to let our appetites sharpen, in accordance with the feeling in consequence of such an expedient to mortify us.

INTERESTING READING—CONTENTS OF A REBEL MAIL, WHICH AFFORDS THE FIRST IDEA TO SOME OF THE PRISONERS AS TO THE CAUSE OF THEIR ARREST—ONE OF MR. SEWARD'S DESPATCHES AMONG REBEL PRISONERS IN FORT-LA-FAYETTE AND BALTIMORE REBEL LADIES—MORE LADY VISITORS TO THE FORT—"THE BONNIE BLUE FLAG," AND "I LOVE OLD DIXIE, RIGHT OR WRONG," BY PRISONERS.

WE have quite interesting reading matter just now in the contents of a Rebel Mail, as published in the newspapers, a portion of which explains the cause of the Irish merchant being sent down. There is no doubt of his being a sympathizer, and it looks very much like, that he has a taste for the adventures of the Blockade business.

We have been most absorbed in the contents of a copy of a despatch of Mr. Seward to Lord Lyons, received by our friend the British Officer here, for associating with disloyal Baltimore ladies. It is quite a lengthy document, covering four pages of what it is to be presumed is his diplomatic post paper, as it is larger than any we have seen for a long time.

According to the amount of writing it is a most formidable document, but all that appears as substance, is an evidence of the Secretary's desire to frighten our young friend, and for ever deter him from becoming a victim to the influence of the bewitching Rebel ladies of Baltimore. He is informed that before there is time for carrying into effect suitable measures for bringing to justice his Baltimore associates, his case cannot be further entertained; and that he (Mr. Seward) will have pleasure in finding that in the meantime Her Britannic Majesty has deemed an officer so guilty as unworthy to carry her commission.

We are not so much surprised at learning his views as to punishment for associating with Baltimore Rebel ladies, as Mr. Seward would doubtless be if he was aware that a complete copy of his despatch was subject to their criticism in a very few days after it was written. We trust that it reached them in time to serve a good purpose.

The holiday season appears to have brought an increase of Lady Visitors to the Officers of the garrison, and occasionally some are included whose object evidently is to have it to say that they had ocular demonstration of the appearance Rebels in prison make, especially, we presume, young good-looking Generals.

Without denying the right of some of us to special admiration, the aggregate of gallantry is such, that whenever either of the Generals are called for by the Officer of the day, while there are ladies in the Fort, especially when the Band is on the parapet, we all make ourselves visible. We cannot, however, appreciate the taste of having us brought out from our comfortable fire, by "Dixie" from the Band, to be immediately followed by "Yankee Doodle," and shall therefore continue to cultivate our voices by rendering "The Bonnie Blue Flag," and "I love Old Dixie, right or wrong," for the benefit of our Yankee Lady Visitors.

EXCITEMENT IN CONSEQUENCE OF A VESSEL AT-
TEMPTING TO PASS BEFORE BEING EXAMINED—
MORE LOYAL CITIZENS BROUGHT DOWN AS
PRISONERS—ADDITIONAL RESTRICTIONS AS TO
VISITORS—THE BLOCKADE RUN WITH GREEN-
BACKS FOR PRISONERS—TRADING THEM WITH
YANKEE SOLDIERS—SUCCESSFUL STRATEGY IN
GETTING NEW CLOTHES.

FOR the first time since the excitement about the supposed attempt to escape by our Georgia friend (who is still in close confinement), and the shock to the nerves to Colonel Burke, from finding the old knife with the gapped edge, we have had, what we have all been wishing for, another excitement in the Fort. It has arisen from a report having reached the Commander of the large number of United States armed vessels, which have been engaged in blockading the harbour since the case of the Cheseapeake, against vessels leaving, as she did, with rebels on board, that a steamer was attempting to get by the Fleet and Forts without submitting to search. The Revenue Cutter at Staten Island signalised—in answer, all the Forts beat to quarters immediately. The guns of the vessels were run out double shotted. Around us the excitement was intense, prisoners being driven in and locked up hours earlier than usual. We thought of Rebel Rams, and all that kind of thing, but it was only a vessel, the captain of which was not aware of the new regulations of the port.

The second week of the new year has brought us hardly anything new. The weather continues extremely cold, which we regret more on account of our lady visitors than ourselves, as we have free access to a pile of good coal, and the cells are so crowded that the want of fresh air at night is most felt. The additional responsibilities to Colonel Burke, since our last, have been a custom-house officer and three other defrauders of the United States Government. The four worthy Unionists have been given select accommodation, in close confinement. The Visiting Officer reports that they were captured when on the point of leaving the country. Charge—altering receipts, by substituting by figures greater for a less number of packages furnished by them as Naval

Contractors. In addition to them, the number in other parts of the Fort have been increased by parties who, under late laws as to defrauders of recruits, are termed "bounty jumpers," which, as understood here, means those who procure substitutes and recruits, have them mustered into service, and retain their money. The reports which reach us across the sentinel lines are, that one of the two who are here already had taken advantage of a sister-in-law, the other of a mother-in-law; and that there is one to come down, who, by holding on to a bounty, was cheating his grandmother.

The addition to the number of loyal citizen prisoners having increased the applications for ladies to visit their relatives in the Fort—and as there are (as it appears) more than the Officers on duty can attend to, and strictly carry out the rules in regard to them—the General in Chief Command has given orders to have withdrawn the privilege to our young Maryland friend to visit her father twice a week, so as to place her on a footing with the Yankee ladies who have husbands in confinement; the consequence being that, under the new rules, our lady friends have to make applications anew each time they require permission to enter the Fort.

Rebellious as our lady friends had a good right to be heretofore, the new restrictions have left no grounds whatever for scruples; the consequence has been that, through our young Maryland Confederate, the inmates of Nos. 2 and 3 have become possessed of means so that under an arrangement to give a Yankee soldier a dollar greenback in exchange for a pound of butter or sugar, and in proportion for other articles equally appreciated under existing circumstances, they are once more within reach of something better than what the most benign government on earth considers good enough for rebels.

Our pickets and scouts are out the moment the doors of our cells are open in the morning, to pick up whatever our Yankee guardians have thought proper to leave at appointed places during the night, as value for greenback money passed to them, while on duty in front of the cells, the previous evening. We cannot complain if it occurs that the result of our outlay is to be seen in a staggering soldier—we do not complain whenever it has the additional effect of getting them in the guardhouse, but would, of course, prefer that it should be the Libbey prison instead.

Yankee garments are to be seen in wear, by those with the most limited wardrobes, when the orders came from Washington not to permit prisoners who had no relatives in New York to get anything outside what the garrison furnished. The greater number of Southerners have felt little inconvenience in that respect. Our Maryland friends put in practice stratagy which even in the course of the present war cannot have been thought of by any one else, by which some gentlemen were saved the mortification of valuing on the gratuity of enemies. It was strictly according to rule for a prisoner having relatives in New York to order for his use a change of under and over-clothes, stockings, and shoes, but the rule did not guard against the contingency of the articles being for the use of others, or of exchanges on account of misfits, in doing which an old wornout garment might be sent to make a package supposed to contain new articles returned to get fitting ones in their stead, and as it has turned out, our Maryland friend could not be fitted until after several trials.

MORE PRISONERS—FINANCIAL OPERATION BETWEEN A PRISONER AND THE UNITED STATES AUTHORITIES—THE (SUPPOSED) HEAD OF THE SOLDIER-DEFRAUDING FRATERNITY BROUGHT DOWN—HE IS THOROUGHLY UNION, AND ELECTED A MEMBER OF CONGRESS, WHO IS TO GET HIM OUT—INVITATION TO YANKEES FOUND IN THE SOUTH WHEN THE WAR IS OVER.

THERE is not much to give under the historic head this week. A couple of supposed rebel soldiers and two more bounty-jumpers have been added to the number in the other part of the Fort.

A bounty-jumper was taken to New York under an arrangement that his father was to endorse his note in favour of the United States for the sum of which he had defrauded the widow of his brother by not giving but a share of the money he had received as bounty for her son; but it appears that the old man thought better of it, and let his son be remanded to board at the expense of his Government for a while longer. One of the jumpers brought down is really a character in himself, a Simon Pure Yankee, with the New York polish, which we presume he must have got in the second-hand furniture line, as he reports such as his legitimate business. He is one of those always-smiling fellows, can't be made to notice the many attempts at amusement at his expense by his rebel room-mates, who appear to have no hesitation in showing that they appreciate him even less than the others of his tribe, which is on account of his evident desire to assume among them the character of a Union Lecturer. He is confident of not only getting a release, but also a clearing-up of his character as soon as a certain Member of Congress—who, he says, is indebted to his influence for his election—is properly made aware of the particulars of his case. He is particularly interested in endeavouring to prove that the time must come, when the war is over, in which he can meet acquaintances in the South same as he did heretofore; and in moralising with our Virginian rebel-captain, presumed without fear of dissent on his part, that as he, as a Yankee, would not hesitate to invite the now rebel-captain to the hospitalities of his house when peace comes, neither would the captain think of the present time when once more in the enjoyment of peace, his smile was not in the least changed when he heard that, as his countrymen had left his rebel-captain acquaintance without a home, he could not possibly be invited to it when the war was over, but that it was certain that if ever he was known to be in his neighbourhood he would invite him to the limb of the first tree to which he could be hung. Still, at the close of the controversy, the Union saver would not allow himself to believe that such feelings attached to more than isolated cases of those who are sacrificing life and property so lavishly for the avowed purpose of getting rid of the Yankee character for ever.

Arrival of a Military Commission for Trial of Prisoners—Additional Restrictions—Orders for Visitors to be Searched—Officer's Object, Order Withdrawn—Excitement in the Fort—Anticipated Attempt to Release Prisoners—Neither Catholic Newspapers nor Episcopal Prayer Books Allowed—Proceedings of the Military Commission—How a New York Silver-Grey Democrat Wanted to Bet—What a Jersey Democrat Would be Glad to Hear—Discharge of British Subjects—The Yankee Policy as to British Blockade Runners.

Our lady friends succeeded in getting a special permit, under which they made one visit this week, instead of two as under the pass withdrawn. As the weather is now, we are uneasy for their safety, as sometimes it is dangerous to attempt crossing from Fort Hamilton, on account of the drifting ice.

The last has been an unusually interesting week. The long looked for Military Commission arrived—made arrangements for an examination into the cases of all the prisoners, with the exception of those known to be in the public service of the Confederate Government, and are expected down on Monday to enter upon their duty.

The last time our lady friends came they were allowed to send, for the use of the prisoners in Cells No. 2 and 3, grace-hoops, handballs, and some ballad music. On the day following their visit, an order was issued to search all visitors to the Fort, and a report got currency that a general search of the prisoners' quarters was about to be started. The greenbacks in No. 2 were hid for a while in a rat hole, and those belonging to No. 3 were for a time in a coal bucket. The "Right Flanker" was suitably looked after, and for two days we would trust none but our most experienced and reliable scouts, to report as to what was transpiring. It is a great relief to find that the danger has not only passed, but that our Maryland lady friends were not the cause of raising the suspicion that something contraband had been going on. It was nevertheless feared at one time that we would have to dispense with their visits, as our Maryland friend properly objected to their being subjected to the indignity of being searched. It may have been on this account, or the fact that the junior officers declined to assist in carrying out such an order, that it was revoked, and a restriction adopted in its stead of limiting interviews between prisoners and those visiting them to strictly half an hour.

As prisoners will do, we have often speculated as to what unexpected occurrence we might possibly owe our delivery from Fort-la-Fayette. Confederate iron-clads, or rams from Europe, or an English or French blockading fleet were thought of, but the idea of such a thing as a premeditated attack on the Forts in the harbour by a force from New York never occurred to us. But it appears it must have to the authorities in New York and the officers here, as about nine o'clock last night we were delighted with the idea that something in the way of a real excitement had occurred. The whole garrison was beat to quarters, guns double-shotted, and pointed so as to cover every possible approach from the city or the Long Island shore. Howitzers covering the doors of the place where there were prisoners, &c.,

&c. Some had it that the appearance of the much-dreaded rams had caused the excitement; others, that the long-talked of time, when the Seymour men of New York would require him to make good his promise to protect them against the Lincoln despotism had arrived. But morning came for us to find that it was even a greater scare than the previous one, as at this time it all arose from the waving of handkerchiefs to some of the prisoners who happened to be in sight when a steamer passed that evening, having on board some lately released British sailors. The movement having been observed from some of the Forts, telegraphic notice went to head-quarters in New York, and from there Colonel Burke was ordered to prepare to repel an attack for the purpose of liberating his prisoners.

This week our Maryland friend was allowed but one interview, and that for only half an hour, with his daughter and her friend, and, having found the strict lieutenant, before alluded to, as officer of the day, They were compelled to take back a copy of a Democratic Catholic paper *(The Metropolitan Record)*, to which our

Maryland friend had been a subscriber for several years; and also an Episcopal Prayer Book, which they brought for a room-mate of his.

The Commissioners have entered upon their duties, but, judging from their examinations so far, it appears that it is to be nothing more nor less than a humbug got up for the purpose of closing the mouths of those in the United States who occasionally find fault with the locking up of people without an examination into the charges against them. The commencement has been with those captured as blockade-runners, the Commissioners knowing so little about their cases that they had to ask information from the prisoners themselves as to the name of the vessel they were on board of, and that of the one they were captured by. After being informed of which, the parties, if holding no position of importance, the question was, "Are you willing to take an oath of allegiance to the United States?" And in the cases of persons of position in the South, "Would you, in the event of the Federal army occupying the place where your family is, still adhere to the Confederate Government?" In respect to the Union citizens, some of the questions have been, to our old grey-headed room-mate, " Have you ever wagered that General Lee would be in Washington by a certain time?" and to our Jersey room-mate, " Have you not been heard to say, on a railroad train, that you would be glad if the rebels would drive the whole abolition crew out of Washington?"

Our Maryland friend has had but to acknowledge the genuineness of a communication in his name, made shortly after his arrest, to the Secretary of War, in which the ground was taken that as no charge against him more than sympathy with the cause of the South could be proven, the Government ought at least to allow him to leave the country.

The only one who has had thus far any reason to hope for result from his examination is the New York merchant who made the bet that he would not be detained here more than a week. It is nearly a month since the inmates of No. 3 had the benefit of fifty dollars in cigars from his loss of that bet, but we are duly glad that he has now a prospect. He has but a cough to complain of; and although rebel-citizens were denied the services of a dentist a short time since, there is no reason why the Judge-Advocate of the Commission should not allow a Union-citizen to get within reach of medical attendance by a removal to the city.

Two of the inmates of No. 3, finding in the course of their examination that the Commissioners had some knowledge of an attempted arrangement on their part by which they could have got away from the Deputy United States Marshal when being conveyed through New York previous to their being brought down here, felt justified in acknowledging that they would have been allowed to escape had they been willing to increase their offer of money. At first they thought that it was benefitting their cases to make the exposure, but after being called several times before the Judge-Advocate, they have concluded that our room-mate, with the cough and a couple of hundred thousand dollars, is the only one who has the least chance of getting out just now.

The week has given us considerable that is new to talk over. Several British subjects have been released; but they were those alone who, in justice, should have been discharged before they were brought here, as the same evidence to their being neutrals was as well known when they were in Ludlow Street Jail as it was when they were let go. However, it is entirely the business of their Government, if it allows the Yankee authorities to take their own time in deciding who they are justified in holding. And it appears not to have come to the knowledge of the British Consul that the captains of Yankee blockaders do not hesitate to say that the purpose is to make all the Englishmen they capture serve at least a couple of months in prison in order to deter them from engaging anew in the blockade trade.

Removal of Confederate Officers to another Fort—Two escape on the way—Anticipated Departure of Two others for their homes: Entertainment in their Honour—Editorial Banquet of the "Right Flanker"—The Sensation of the Day:—"Braves, who have with Stonewall bled!" for the First Time.

The Officers comprising the staff of the General brought here some time since from New Orleans, and two other Confederate Officers, were started under guard for Fort McHenry. The mail which brought information of the arrival of the Staff Officers at their place of destination, brought to us the welcome news that the plans of the other two to escape on the way had been entirely successful. One having relieved the guard of the care of him near the railway depôt in Jersey City, and the other near the depôt in Baltimore. Before starting, there was something mentioned in respect to their giving parole of honour while on the train, but as it was decided by them not to come under an obligation of the kind, our friends are all right, if they can only properly disguise themselves, and keep out of the way of detective officers.

The No. 3 party, who have got along so pleasantly together, is to be further reduced shortly by the removal of two, the return of whom to their country and families will be hailed with the greatest pleasure, at the same time that the loss of their companionship will be regretted by all. We trust that their cases, and those of the two held so long as hostages for them, may be the last expedient of the kind during the war.

In view of their leaving, and the fact of our having been in possession of funds enough to give an entertainment, in conformity with the estimate in which they have been held by all as friends of the "Right Flanker" enterprise, and some old rye being at disposal, yesterday was availed of as an occasion suitable for our local item reporter getting up an account of what had been in contemplation some time, but which has been delayed in hopes of our having it in our power to be better prepared for such an affair; a sensational account *(à la Herald)* of an Editorial Banquet in honour of the "Right

Flanker." The report of such a banquet appears in our local item column as follows :

"The Sensation of the Day."
"The great Editorial Banquet of the 'Right Flanker.'"
"The La-Fayette Bastile in a Blaze of Glory."
"Great Concentration of Patriotism."
"The Programme of the Only Way to End the War."
"The Emperor of China (the owner of the Anglo-Rebel Rams) to arbitrate."
"The Knights of the Golden Circle."
"Pass-word—'Cousin Sally Ann,'" &c., &c.

Extract :—The Great Editorial Banquet of the "Right Flanker" at the La-Fayette Bastile.—This much-talked-of and long-expected entertainment came off yesterday with great éclat. The company present on the occasion included the most notable and fashionable of the sojourners at that celebrated establishment. The sentimental, and other tastes, evidenced, were such, that we can say, after an experience derived from an attendance at all the reunions of a similar nature which have taken place in that abode of fashion, such a treat for the admirers of patriotism has never been equalled, and, as might have been anticipated, ideas were called forth which could only be looked for in an assembly of the kind. The preparations for the gratification of epicurean taste was the result of the most careful attention on the part of the caterer, whose ability in that respect had been frequently tested by similar occasions. It was generally conceded that it was out of his power to have succeeded more admirably. As usual of late the tables were furnished exclusively from the productions for which the Bastile estate has so long been famous. In fact, it might be said that every want was supplied from the establishment itself, as it became necessary to procure elsewhere but one article in the liquor line.

The chair was most appropriately filled, and at about four o'clock the festivities commenced by a suggestion from the Chairman that it would be in good taste and appropriate to the occasion to preface the regular toasts with a suitable recognition of the esteem in which those present held such an illustrious personage, and he therefore proposed the health of His Majesty *the Emperor of China*. As might be anticipated, the mere mention of the name had the effect looked for, as such a means of awakening pleasant reminiscences of home, and the cheering only subsided to give way to the band which struck up " Carry me back to old Virginia."

The senior Editor furnished the first regular toast—" The ' Right Flanker ;' may its position be ever impregnable in connection with a centre, having *a Lee in front* and *the memory of a Jackson in the rear*, and may the *left rest on Southern Independence*," which brought out the most successful effort of the Musical Club in attendance in singing—

> Braves who have with Stonewall bled
> Braves whom Lee hath ofttimes led,
> Welcome to your gory bed,
>   Or to victory.
>
> Now's the day and now's the hour,
> See the front of battle lower,
> See approach Lincoln's power,
>   Chains and slavery.

> Who would be a traitor knave?
> Who could fill a coward's grave?
> Who so base as be a slave?
> > Let him turn and flee.
>
> Who for Southern rights and laws
> Freedom's sword will bravely draw,
> Freeman stand or Freeman fall,
> > Let him on with Lee.
>
> By oppressions, woes, and pains,
> By our sires in dungeons chained,
> We will drain our dearest veins,
> > But they shall be free.
>
> Lay the base usurpers low,
> Tyrants fall in every foe,
> Liberty's in every blow,
> > Let us do or die.

Then followed "The Right Flanker;" its principles and its policy: undying faith in our glorious cause, and the advocation of every effort for our liberty." *Music*—"The Bonnie Blue Flag."

"May peace be the source of as much glory as the war has been, and our poets rival our warriors." *Music*—"Juanita."

"The life-drama we are now enacting: may the curtain fall and rise no more on the same performance." *Music*—"Annie Laurie."

"The Southern Army, a band of patriots struggling for liberty; they will never succumb to Northern tyranny." *Music*—"Stonewall Jackson's March."

"Raphael Semmes, the pioneer cruiser of the Confederate Navy: may he live to triumph on the ocean while the war lasts, and to enjoy the fruits of his labour when peace is established." *Music*—"A Life on the Ocean Wave."

"The day we celebrate, as distance in the landscape lends enchantment to the view; so, in other days and other climes, we'll gladly think of you." *Music*—"Home, Sweet Home."

After the announcement of the regular toasts, and the discussion of the merits of what was intended to promote a flow of soul, the next in order were volunteer toasts, which were as follows:—

"Our Chairman, the worthy son of one of the most famous in upholding the honour of the Old Dominion in the greatest rebellion of ancient or modern times." *Music*—"Hail to the Chief."

"The Hero in the nautical exploit which,

more than any other, has proved what can be expected from a navy which, in infancy, has the last chance for life volunteered in its service." *Music*—" The Confederate March."

" The Representatives of the Heroes to whom is entrusted the defence of our soil, the confidence of such men as have been tested at Vicksburg and Port Hudson, is not to be shaken by the trials of Fort-la-Fayette." *Music*—" Beauregard's March."

" The Pioneers in the Foreign Trade of the Confederate States." *Music*—" Up with the Stars and the Bars."

" The right kind of Allies for the Confederacy, such as are present from the lands of the Shamrock and Thistle. To fight its cause with pen and sword is all the privilege they want." *Music*—" St. Patrick's Day," and " The Campbells are Coming."

" The Maryland Blue Eyes, which so frequently look down upon the evidence of the struggle in which her native State has so much interest—the present Captives in Fort-la-Fayette." *Music*—" Maryland, my Maryland."

" Sweethearts and Wives," and " Cousin

Sally-Ann," were given at the conclusion ; and at about five o'clock the company was broken up—the members (including the writer) returning to their respective homes to enjoy the pleasure of reflecting that had they not been in attendance they would have lost such an opportunity as cannot be expected to occur again.

A TRIFLING ARTICLE DENIED A PRISONER—NEWS FROM THE ESCAPED PRISONERS—ONE HAS A PLEASANT TIME IN WESTERN VIRGINIA, BALTIMORE, NEW YORK, AND BOSTON, BEFORE LEAVING FOR BERMUDA—LEAVING OF TWO PRISONERS FOR FORTRESS MONROE, TO BE EXCHANGED—THE PROCEEDINGS OF THE MILITARY COMMISSION CONCLUDED—THE ONLY RESULT THE TRANSFER OF A RICH UNION CITIZEN TO A NEW YORK JAIL.

No one has been discharged yet in consequence of examination by the Military Commissioners. Our Maryland friend had an interview this week of just the half-hour with his daughter, and in consequence of the late strictness in other respects, he was not allowed to receive a trifling article brought him as a birth-day gift.

The principal subject of interest during the week has been the report from our friend the Officer who escaped at the depôt at Baltimore. When jokingly talking over the chances of escape, his room-mates suggested as a programme, to be followed in case of success in getting away from the guard, first to assume the character of a preacher, on account of delicate appearance. Secondly, if some tracts should be within reach, to be sure and have a good supply to hand round among railway or steamer passengers. Not to omit having at all times in hand a good Abolition Newspaper (the *New York Tribune*, if possible,) and campaign it so with passengers adjoining that the rebellion be crushed in not over 30 days, and that Jefferson Davis and all his followers come to the gallows as soon as possible afterwards. Then, so soon as out of danger, to insert a personal in the *Herald*, using certain cabalistic words, which were on the walls of the cell, as we would be on the look out. We are not aware of his having had recourse to the tracts, *Tribune*, speedy crushing of the rebellion, and hanging all the Rebels; but we have the personal in the *Herald*, from which it appears he went out from the Capes of Virginia in a British vessel.

The other lucky fellow, who escaped at the Jersey City Depôt, not having been a roommate of the editorial staff of the "Right Flanker," failed to inform us exactly of the programme of his case, still *we know* that after relieving his keepers of all responsibility on his account, he passed quite a pleasant time in Western Virginia, Maryland, New York, and Boston, before leaving for Halifax and Bermuda.

Next to the cases of our escaped friends, the two hostages have left for Fortress Monroe to be exchanged. We missed them from the spots occupied by them in our small quarters for several months of the (to us) long winter season. May all the happiness they wished for attend their arrival home.

The Military Commissioners appeared to have concluded their labours, and as we learn started for Fort Warren; the only result being the removal of our fellow-prisoner with the bad cough, and the two hundred thousand dollars, to a jail in New York, from which we hear that he is allowed to be absent nightly, by paying an officer to accompany him. We sincerely congratulate him. Prisoners may not feel for every one who is brought down here, at the same time it is invariably the case that all are glad to see any one regain liberty.

THE MILITARY COMMISSIONERS AND A CONFEDERATE ENGINEER; THE LATTER CONTENDS THAT THERE IS A CONFEDERATE GOVERNMENT, FOR WHICH HE IS MORE CLOSELY LOCKED UP—A JAR OF OYSTERS DENIED A PRISONER.

THE last act performed by the Commissioners proved to be in accordance with our ideas, as to the whole operation, on their part, being a farce. Among the number examined by them, some of whom were before them more than once, were several attached to the engine department of a captured blockade-runner. These were called up, and offered their liberty provided they were willing to exercise their capacities in the service of the Government. On a proposition of the kind being made to the chief-engineer (a Baltimorean), the remark was made by him that he was already in Government employ, whereupon the officers concluded that they must have been trying a loyal citizen, and were about to order a discharge of the supposed injured party, until he informed them that it was the Confederate Government he alluded to, when he received an extra reprimand for the expression of the word Government, as applied by him, and was quickly remanded to his cell.

Our Maryland friend had a visit from his ladies (for the half hour) this week, also from a Holland friend of his, who, not knowing the rules of the Fort, brought for him a jar of pickled oysters. But, strange as it to us appears, on account of our knowledge of the apparent preference which the Colonel has for him (our Maryland room-mate), he would not allow him to receive the jar of oysters. Perhaps it is owing to the proprietor of the restaurant where the oysters were purchased, the same who some time since objected to a package of game for a prisoner here being directed to him in the place where he did not hesitate to receive the money for them.

A Union Prisoner's Appeal for Vegetables—His Relatives fear that his Mind is Affected—His hope on account of Rothschilds' Agent hanging out the Old Flag, and helping to Crush the Rebellion—Controversies between Northern Citizens as to the Standard for Society—Difference of Treatment to Union and Rebel Prisoners.

THE interest which the past week has afforded outside, of local items and the ordinary contributions to our columns, has been in the case of our room-mate from New Jersey. For some time he, like many of us, has been suffering in health from the want of vegetable matter, and has frequently endeavoured to sufficiently impress the friends to whom he wrote, with the idea that he could not possibly survive much longer under the present restrictions as to food. An unfavourable turn of feelings in mind, as well as body, induced him a few nights since to be influenced by a room-mate having a waggish taste, who suggested that an application to head-quarters for enough of vegetable matter *to smell*, instead of to eat, would be attended with success, and he therefore directed his lady-friends to make such an application. As soon as they received a request from him for a "few small potatoes and an onion," they concluded that his mind had become affected, and, while under the excitement such an idea occasioned, procured a permit, not for one alone as heretofore, but for three of them to visit him. The result of such a visit, under such circumstances, can be more easily imagined than described. We are happy to say, however, that their alarm was uncalled for, as the only time our room-mate appeared at all unreasonable has been when in the expectation that, in consequence of his brother-in-faith, the agent of the Rothschilds, having always a large silk star-spangled banner displayed from a Fifth Avenue residence, and the fact of his having done so much in means towards crushing the rebellion, he (our Jersey room-mate) ought to receive favourable attention at the hands of the Government. Occasionally he and our New York Democratic room-mate would become excited in controversy in enlightening us rebels as to the standard of society in the Empire City: one contending that a great bridge-builder was at the head, as he had the most money; while the other granted that privilege to the man who could afford to present to the Government a steamer to catch the Alabama. With these exceptions, we have found our Jersey room-mate always inclined to keep within discretionary limits, after making proper allowance for the latitude as the inventor of the "endless chains of fire," all must agree he is entitled to.

The late New York hotel-keeper, lastly (as we are given to understand) occupying a high position among the bounty-jumpers, having adopted the sick-stratagy—as did our No. 3 rich Union room-mate, who is now under medical care in New York—has been allowed to order in delicacies from his lady-relatives; while so strict are the rules in respect to us rebels and rebel-sympathisers, that of late our musket-carrying guardians can't operate at the rate of a pound of butter or a pound of sugar for a dollar of the green-backs which our young lady friend took so much risk in bringing us. She and her companion have been down as usual this week, and we are most happy to find that they give encouraging accounts as to efforts which are being made by the friends of the special object of their visits towards having him turned over to the jurisdiction of a Civil Court in New York, it having been decided that he is not guilty of a military offence.

THE STRONG ARMS AND BRAVE HEARTS OF THEIR COUNTRYMEN THE ONLY DEPENDENCE OF REBEL PRISONERS—ANTICIPATED NECESSITY FOR DISCONTINUANCE OF THE "RIGHT FLANKER"—REMOVAL OF SEVERAL PRISONERS FROM THE FORT, AND THE EXISTING COPIES OF IT ENTRUSTED TO THEM—FINAL DISCONTINUANCE OF IT—PUBLICATION OF FORT-LA-FAYETTE LIFE.

FINE March weather keeps us out of doors more than usual, and though allowed an increase of room to exercise in, we feel the confinement more unbearable than when the weather obliged us to stay more indoors. And as it is now settled that nothing favourable is to result from the examination by the Military Commission, we have nothing to look to but the holding out of our health, and patience, and the strong arms and brave hearts of our fellow-countrymen.

Since four of the original inmates of No. 3, and three from No. 2, have been removed, the number of reliable Right Flankers have not only become considerably less, but in some instances the places of the friends of the enterprise are occupied by doubtful parties. It therefore becomes necessary to exercise unusual caution, in doing which the result of our efforts must naturally be lessened. This explanation is made for the information of the readers at the other side, who notice that their communications do not appear this week.

The only change among the prisoners has been in the removal of the Captain and Officers of a captured steamer to a jail in New York, to serve as witnesses in deciding whether a Government transport which made the capture, or the regular cruiser which came up shortly afterwards, is entitled to the prize money.

Our lady friends down as usual, bringing the gratifying news that a friend from Washington reports that an order is out to remove our Maryland room-mate to the jurisdiction of a Court in New York.

As the remaining Right Flankers are about to retire for the night, the officer of the day is in Cell No. 3, to report that early in the morning our Maryland room-mate, the three others arrested at the time he was, and our young friend who was brought here from the Capitol Prison, are to be removed to head quarters. As their baggage includes some trunks well adapted for the purpose of secreting considerable bulk, and as there does not remain an effective force to get up another issue of the " Right Flanker," it is determined that the occasion be availed of to remove the existing copies of it from Fort-la-Fayette. The idea, in part, in getting up such a sheet as the " Right Flanker," having been for the purpose of interest to, and reference by, those who have been or may be inmates of Fort-la-Fayette, as well as to afford those who have not had an opportunity to judge correctly as to Life in it. It is presumed not improbable that the interest of readers in the present Extracts will be increased by an addition to explain the course in regard to persons liberated from there who have not a status under the cartel for exchange of prisoners between the United and Confederate States authorities.

It is therefore thought proper first to refer to the cases of the five who, left in charge of the last issues of the " Right Flanker," which is done as briefly as possible to be correct and just. After removal from the charge of the officers in command of the Fort, the five prisoners alluded to were taken to the Major-General commanding the department. The one whose parole had been ignored when he was sent down was allowed the privilege of it again ; the other four were sent to a jail, subject to the United States Civil Authorities, from which, after some detention, they were released by entering into bonds for appearance before an United States Commissioner, who, after hearing all the evidence in possession of the Washington Authorities, ordered a final release on the grounds (as near as understood) that, according to law, parties *merely agreeing to aid* another, who did not actually intend to commit an offence (and the Detective swore that he did not), were not amenable under any known statute. The result, of course, was taken advantage of as soon as possible by the released parties—the captain returning to the command of his vessel ; the patent fusé manufacturer to look up the best customer for his invention, he being again at liberty (he had always been willing) to let the highest bidder have it.

The chief of the Silver-Grey Democrats (as he, in the Fort, termed the party of which he claimed to be the head), from appearances, assumed the place of a martyr, although he had not a single friend or relative to make him a visit during an incarceration of five months; and the Marylander became free to renew his business as a merchant.

It is not known how the movements of three of the four finally resulted, but a special interest in the Marylander, on account of the peculiar result in his case, causes it to be noticed in "Fort-la-Fayette Life." Soon after getting his liberty, without coming under obligations to the United States Government, he was so unlucky as to become compromised again in efforts to save a friend from conscription into the Yankee service, making an immediate departure for neutral territory necessary.

Only those who have endured the trials and hardships of a prison life, can best appreciate the blessings of personal liberty. And, therefore, the meeting of exiles in a friendly country was the occasion of congratulation and the source of much interest. Especially when, as in the present instance, several were of the editorial staff of the "Right Flanker." Many of the exiles had been confined in various Federal prisons; some had just arrived from Fort-la-Fayette, and brought tidings of the remaining editorial corps yet within its gloomy cells.

One of them, a captain, had plunged boldly into the sea from its walls, upon a dark and stormy night, with a life-preserver around him, which his friends had procured in a contraband manner, and having floated with the tide, landed on the beach some three miles distant from the Fort. Another, a contributor to the "Flanker," had been released, after his long incarceration, as the Secretary of State and Her Majesty's representative had at length arrived at the conclusion that he was innocent of the charges made against him.

It was then determined to publish extracts from the "Right Flanker," as affording a correct knowledge of prison life in the United States during the present war, and properly enlightening the public at large in regard to subjects of special interest to them.

www.ingramcontent.com/pod-product-compliance
Lightning Source LLC
Chambersburg PA
CBHW031406160426
43196CB00007B/913